MARGRET & H.A. REY'S

Curious George

and the Puppies

Illustrated in the style of H. A. Rey by Vipah Interactive

Houghton Mifflin Harcourt
Boston   New York

Copyright © 1998 by Houghton Mifflin Harcourt Publishing Company

Based on the character of Curious George®, created by Margret and H. A. Rey.
Illustrated by Vipah Interactive: C. Becker, D. Fakkel, M. Jensen, S. SanGiacomo, C. Yu.

Curious George® is a registered trademark of Houghton Mifflin Harcourt Publishing Company

hmhbooks.com

The text of this book is set in 17-pt. Adobe Garamond.
The illustrations are watercolor and charcoal pencil, reproduced in full color.

Library of Congress Cataloging-in-Publication Data
Curious George and the puppies / based on the original character by Margret and H. A. Rey.
p.   cm.
Summary: Curious George goes to the animal shelter where he accidentally lets all the dogs
out of their cages and creates quite a ruckus.
[1. Monkeys—Fiction. 2. Animals—Fiction.]   I. Rey, Margret, 1906–1996.
II. Rey, H. A. (Hans Augusto), 1898–1977.
PZ7.C92123   1998
[E]—dc21   97-50444
                                                               CIP
                                                                AC

ISBN: 978-0-358-15722-9

Manufactured in China
SCP 10 9 8 7 6 5 4 3 2 1
4500764907

This is George.

George was a good little monkey and always very curious.

One day George went for a walk with his friend, the man with the yellow hat.

When they sat down to rest, they noticed a tiny kitten peeking out from under a bush. The kitten looked frightened.

"Perhaps she is lost," said the man with the yellow hat.

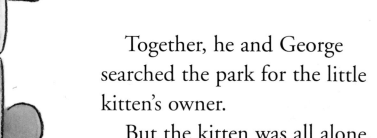

Together, he and George searched the park for the little kitten's owner.

But the kitten was all alone.

"This kitten is too young to be on her own," the man said. "We should take her to the animal shelter, where they can care for her and find her a home."

So George and the kitten and the man with the yellow hat drove to the animal shelter.

The director of the shelter was glad to see them. "It was good of you to bring the kitten here," she said. "We will be happy to take care of her."

George gave the kitten to the director, then he and the man with the yellow hat walked inside.

"Come in," the director said, "but watch where you step. We have a large litter of puppies and one has gotten out of his cage. We're still looking for him, so please be careful."

She closed the door quickly behind them.

George had never been to an animal shelter before. Animals of all kinds were being cared for here. George saw bunnies, cats, turtles, and guinea pigs. He even saw a snake.

But he didn't see any puppies.

"George, I need to sign some papers," said the man with the yellow hat. "Please stay here and don't be too curious."

Just as the man with the yellow hat left the room, George heard barking. Maybe it was the puppies!

But where was it coming from?

George was curious.

He followed the barking noises . . .

and found a room full of dogs! There were yellow dogs, spotted dogs, sleek dogs, and fluffy dogs. There were quiet dogs and yappy dogs and even a dog without a tail. But where were the puppies?

Then George saw a
little wagging tail.

Then another.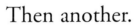

And another!

13

Once George saw the
puppies, he could not take
his eyes off them.
He had to pet one.

Here was a puppy!
The puppy liked George.

George wanted to hold the
puppy. Slowly, he opened the
door . . .

but before George could even reach the puppy, the mother dog
pushed the door open and was off like a shot! George tried to close
the door after her, but the puppies were too fast!

There was nothing George could do.

Puppies were everywhere!

Puppies hid under the desk. Puppies barked at bunnies. One puppy played with a telephone cord and another climbed on top of a cage to watch the others get into mischief.

Soon all the dogs were barking, the cats were meowing, and the bunnies rustled into the corner of their cage.

"Oh no!" cried the director as she and the man with the yellow hat rushed into the room. "Now ALL the puppies are out!"

The man with the yellow hat helped the director gather up the puppies and put them safely back in their cage. Soon all the animals settled down and were quiet.

Except for one.
Who was still barking?
It was the mother dog!
What was she barking at? There was nothing here but a door.

There must be something on the other side, thought George.

He opened the door.

It was the missing puppy! Everyone was happy to finally find the puppy. The director scooped him up and said, "George, you certainly caused a ruckus! But if you hadn't let the puppies out, we might still be searching for this little one."

Then she gave the puppies and their mother a snack.

"These puppies are now big enough to go live with families who will take care of them," she said. "Do you want to take one home with you, George?"

George did.